VOICES FROM AROUND THE WORLD

PACIFIC ISLANDS
NEW ZEALAND

Written by Philippa Werry

with André Ngāpō

NORWOOD HOUSE PRESS

Norwood House Press
For more information about Norwood House Press please visit our website at www.norwoodhousepress.com or call 866-565-2900.
© 2023 Norwood House Press.
All rights reserved. No part of this book may be reproduced or utilized in any form or by any means without written permission from the publisher.

Credits
Editor: Mari Bolte
Designer: Sara Radka

Photo Credits
page 3: ©JBOY / Shutterstock; page 4: ©Fiona Goodall / Stringer / Getty Images; page 5: ©Dimitris66 / Getty Images; page 5: ©Bardocz Peter / Shutterstock; page 5: ©Stewart Watson / Getty Images; page 6: ©LazingBee / Getty Images; page 8: ©CreativeFire / Getty Images; page 9: ©LazingBee / Getty Images; page 10: ©shells1 / Getty Images; page 11: ©Mark Meredith / Getty Images; page 12: ©Hulton Archive / Stringer / Getty Images; page 15: ©Richard001 / Wikimedia; page 16: ©Oliver Strewe / Getty Images; page 17: ©natmint / Getty Images; page 19: ©Jason Oxenham / Stringer / Getty Images; page 20: ©Hulton Archive / Stringer / Getty Images; page 21: ©Sandra Mu / Stringer / Getty Images; page 22: ©Podzemnik / Wikimedia; page 23: ©Ulanwp / Wikimedia; page 25: ©Handout / Getty Images; page 26: ©Hannah Peters / Staff / Getty Images; page 28: ©Blythwood / Wikimedia; page 29: ©Phil Walter / Staff / Getty Images; page 31: ©Matthew Micah Wright / Getty Images; page 32: ©scottespie / Getty Images; page 33: ©MarcelStrelow / Getty Images; page 34: ©Salena Stinchcombe / Shutterstock; page 35: ©Hannah Peters / Staff / Getty Images; page 36: ©chameleonseye / Getty Images; page 38: ©Ricardo Barata / Shutterstock; page 39: ©Chameleons Eye Witness / Newscom; page 41: ©Matthew Micah Wright / Getty Images; page 42: ©Michael Paler/Actionplus / Newscom; page 43: ©Hayne Palmour Iv/ZUMA Press / Newscom; page 44: ©Blue Planet Studio / Getty Images

Cover: ©nazar_ab / Getty Images; ©xavierarnau / Getty Images; ©Juergen / Shutterstock

Library of Congress Cataloging-in-Publication Data
Names: Werry, Philippa, 1958- author. | Ngāpō, André, consultant.
Title: New Zealand / by Philippa Werry ; consultant, André Ngāpō.
Description: [Chicago] : Norwood House Press, [2023] | Series: Voices from around the world : Pacific Islands | Includes bibliographical references and index. | Audience: Ages 8-10 | Audience: Grades 4-6 | Summary: "The islands of New Zealand are full of rich history and culture. Describes the history, customs, geography, and culture of the people who live there, and provides authentic vocabulary words for an immersive experience. Includes a glossary, index, and bibliography for further reading"-- Provided by publisher.
Identifiers: LCCN 2022018942 (print) | LCCN 2022018943 (ebook) | ISBN 9781684507481 (hardcover) | ISBN 9781684048137 (paperback) | ISBN 9781684048182 (epub)
Subjects: LCSH: New Zealand--Juvenile literature.
Classification: LCC DU408 .W47 2022 (print) | LCC DU408 (ebook) | DDC 993--dc23/eng/20220420
LC record available at https://lccn.loc.gov/2022018942
LC ebook record available at https://lccn.loc.gov/2022018943

Hardcover ISBN: 978-1-68450-748-1
Paperback ISBN: 978-1-68404-813-7

Table of Contents

Welcome to New Zealand **4**

Chapter 1:
The History of New Zealand **6**

Chapter 2:
Island Geography **14**

Chapter 3:
Island Traditions **18**

Chapter 4:
New Zealand Today **30**

    Glossary 46

    Read More about the Pacific Islands 47

    Index 48

GUIDE TO PRONOUNCING TE REO MĀORI VOWELS

A (like c<u>a</u>r)

E (like <u>e</u>gg)

I (like f<u>ee</u>t)

O (like <u>oa</u>r)

U (like y<u>ou</u>)

Welcome to New Zealand

Kia ora! That means "hello" in the Māori language. Māori are the **indigenous** people of New Zealand. Welcoming people is part of their culture.

Two important concepts of Māori life are *manaakitanga* (hospitality, kindness, and support) and *whanaunatanga* (relationship and connection).

Where is New Zealand?

New Zealand has three main islands: North Island, South Island, and Stewart Island.

The Māori have different names for their islands. The most common name for the South Island is Te Waipounamu, or "the *pounamu* (greenstone) waters." The North Island is Te Ika a Māui, or "the fish of Māui."

AOTEAROA

While some call the islands New Zealand, the Māori people call the islands by its original name, Aotearoa. In 2021, the Māori Party started a petition to officially change the name back to Aotearoa.

CHAPTER 1

The History of New Zealand

The Māori have a creation story about how the world began. Ranginui was the sky father and Papatūānuku was the Earth mother. They held each other so tightly that their children had no room to move. They pushed their parents apart. This let in the light.

The **demigod** Māui-pōtiki, commonly called Māui, is credited with bringing the islands out of the sea. Māui was clever and curious. But he liked to play tricks. And he sometimes acted without thinking. He carried a special hook given from his grandparents.

One day, Māui's brothers went fishing without him. But Māui hid in the *waka* (canoe). He caught a giant fish. He pulled and pulled until the fish rose above the surface. That is how Māui fished up the North Island. On a map, the tail of the fish Māui caught is the North Island. The South Island is Māui's canoe. Stewart Island is his anchor stone.

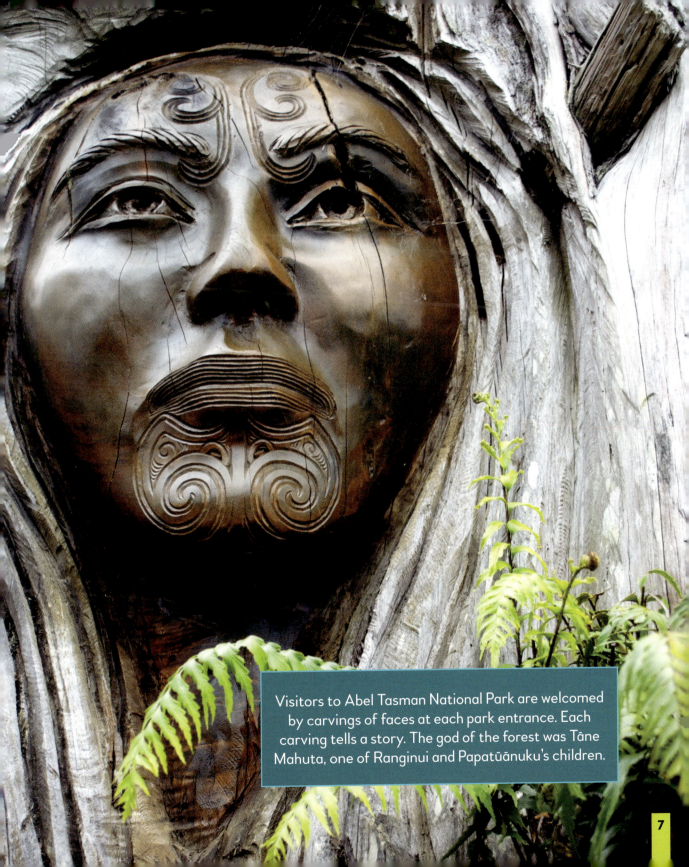

Visitors to Abel Tasman National Park are welcomed by carvings of faces at each park entrance. Each carving tells a story. The god of the forest was Tāne Mahuta, one of Ranginui and Papatūānuku's children.

Curved koru pendants represent the way life both changes and stays the same. Many are made of pounamu.

Today, some people wear a *hei matau* (pounamu pendant) carved in the shape of Māui's hook. Pounamu is a stone. It is also called jade, greenstone, or nephrite. It is found in other countries too. In New Zealand, it is formed high up in the mountains of the South Island. It is washed down the rivers and to the coast.

Pounamu can look like an ordinary stone with a rough outer crust. But when it is cut and polished, it is a beautiful green with specks of other colors. It feels cool but gets warmer as you hold it. The most valuable stones let light shine through.

Māori didn't have metal before the Europeans arrived. Instead, they used different types of stones, especially pounamu, which is hard and tough. They sharpened it and used it to cut down trees and build waka. They carved ornaments and fishing hooks and weapons.

A special piece of pounamu was more than a stone. It was a treasure with its own name and was passed down within a person's *whānau* (family).

Poutini and Pounamu

Poutini was a protective guardian. He took the form of a fierce water creature known as taniwha. He kept the West Coast of the South Island safe. One day, he went north. He saw Waitaiki bathing in the sea. He thought she was very beautiful. Poutini kidnapped her and fled back to the South Island. Waitaiki's husband chased them. Not wanting to give Waitaiki up, Poutini turned her into pounamu. He left her in the Arahura River. Waitaiki became the mother of the pounamu found around the Arahura River. Every piece of greenstone that flows from the river to the sea is her child.

Māori arrived from Polynesia in 1200 to 1300 CE, or about 900 years ago. They quickly learned that pounamu made the perfect tool.

There were no roads. The people made tracks through the **bush** to find the pounamu. These became known as the pounamu or greenstone trails. Families could live off the land for weeks on the trail. They wore sandals made of flax or cabbage tree leaves. The sandals only lasted a few days, but they made new ones as the old ones wore out. Māori traders crossed mountain passes to trade pounamu for other goods with Māori on the other side of the island.

Routeburn Falls is part of an historic greenstone trading route.

Māori were the only people on the islands for centuries. European explorers did not arrive for about 600 years. They didn't know the trails. A Māori man called Kehu knew the country well. He guided the explorer Thomas Brunner and artist Charles Heaphy, both English, through the South Island. Without Kehu, they would never have made their way so far south.

In 1642, Dutchman Abel Tasman sailed past the coast. James Cook, an officer in the British Royal Navy, and his crew on the *Endeavour* were the first Europeans to land in 1769. A Tahitian chief called Tupaia was on Cook's ship. He could communicate with the Māori.

South Island's Milford Sound is known for its rain forests and waterfalls.

DID YOU KNOW?

Europeans often gave names to places that already had Māori names. For example, Cook named Mount Egmont in 1770. Today, though, the mountain is called by its original Māori name, Taranaki.

Māori meeting houses were built before European contact. They were first built as homes for chiefs and later, places to gather.

Many of the first meetings between Māori and Europeans were friendly. But it was often hard to communicate. There were sometimes quarrels and deaths. Māori got sick from new diseases.

In 1840, New Zealand became a colony of Great Britain. Thousands of new **migrants** arrived. The New Zealand Company had promised the new colonists land. It was a private company formed to encourage people to move to the colonies. But the settlers didn't know that the company had made unfair deals to get the land. Fights over who owned the land lasted until 1872. In 1881, government forces invaded Parihaka, a peaceful Māori settlement.

Māori land was stolen. They no longer owned the pounamu. Many precious treasures were removed. Thousands remain in museums overseas today. They include a *whare whakairo* (carved meeting house) in the Field Museum in Chicago.

Some Māori pieces have come home again. The meeting house called Mataatua Wharenui was built in 1875. It was taken to Australia and then England. After 100 years, it was returned and rebuilt in the place where it came from.

Unfair Targets

After World War II (1939–1945), many people immigrated from the Pacific Islands. Most of them needed special permission. But after the permission ended, they became overstayers. In the 1970s, the New Zealand government started to look for overstayers. Police went into factories. They stopped people on the streets. They took dogs and went into houses. These "Dawn Raids" happened early in the morning. Often, people were still in bed. People whose visas had expired were sent back home. There were overstayers from other countries, but the Dawn Raids specifically targeted Pasifika, or people from Pacific Island nations. In 2021, Prime Minister Jacinda Ardern issued a formal apology for the Dawn Raids on behalf of the government.

CHAPTER 2

Island Geography

New Zealand has three main islands. But the country is made up of more than 600 islands in total. About 700 people live on Rēkohu, also known as the Chatham Islands. Some are descendants of the Moriori.

The Moriori are the indigenous people of Rēkohu. They arrived about 600 years ago by canoe from Polynesia and New Zealand. The Moriori were peace-loving people and didn't believe in war or killing. Today, many descendants of these first Moriori still live on Rēkohu.

On Rēkohu, there are many native birds and plants. You can also see dendroglyphs. These are pictures carved into the bark of living trees.

Dendroglyphs are hundreds of years old. Some have been taken away to be cared for in museums. Not all have survived. But we know what they looked like because of Christina Jefferson.

Who was Christina Jefferson?

Christina Jefferson was born in Dunedin on the South Island in 1891. She was interested in history and loved the countryside. In 1947, she went to Rēkohu to look for dendroglyphs. She made six journeys over her lifetime. She traveled hundreds of miles on horseback or on foot. She camped or stayed in huts. Christina found more than 1,000 tree carvings and drew copies of nearly half of them.

Moriori dendroglyphs show people and the things around them.

About 100 million years ago, a land mass called Zealandia broke away from Antarctica. Then, it broke away from Australia. Most of Zealandia is underwater. But New Zealand sticks up out of the sea.

For a long time, there were no predators on the islands. That's why there are so many native animals and birds. The moa was a giant flightless bird. It is extinct now. But you can still see other flightless birds, like the kiwi and kākāpō.

Reptiles called tuatara are the last survivors of a group of creatures that lived in the time of the dinosaurs. Tuatara can live to be 100 years old.

Kiwi are only found in New Zealand.

Pōhutukawa grow best near the sea.

There are also many native trees. The pōhutukawa is called "New Zealand's Christmas tree." Its red flowers come out at Christmastime. Because New Zealand is in the southern hemisphere, Christmas is in summer.

The North Island has volcanoes, geysers, hot springs, and boiling mud pools. The South Island has snow-covered mountains, glaciers, and fjords. Both islands have rivers, lakes, and beaches.

New Zealand sits on the Ring of Fire. This is a chain of volcanoes and earthquakes around the edge of the Pacific Ocean. New Zealand also has many volcanoes and earthquakes. Some earthquakes are only small. But some are big and scary.

CHAPTER 3

Island Traditions

The first person to discover New Zealand might have been the great *Rangatira* (chief), Kupe. Kupe was chasing a giant octopus. As he sailed across the Pacific Ocean, he found an unknown land rising from the sea. His wife, Kuramārōtini, called the new country Ao-tea-roa, or "Land of the Long White Cloud."

After Kupe, the first explorers ventured here from their ancient homeland, Hawaiki in East Polynesia. They used the clues of winds, stars, ocean currents, and migrating birds to steer their waka.

The first Europeans were sailors and explorers. Sealers and whalers followed. Traders set up shops. **Missionaries** opened schools and churches. New settlers arrived in sailing ships. It took months to sail from the other side of the world. But people came. They came from China, India, Italy, Greece, Scandinavia, and Germany. They came from Scotland, England, and Ireland. They were all looking for a new life with new opportunities. In the 20th century, some people came to escape war or as refugees.

Today, most people arrive by plane. But canoes are still used in a sport called waka ama. Other people build voyaging canoes like the ones used to bring their ancestors to New Zealand.

Crews paddled down the Waitangi River in large Māori canoe as part of an annual celebration.

By 1840, British Navy officer William Hobson brought a **treaty** to the Māori chiefs. It was written in English. Some chiefs knew English, but not all. Hobson didn't know any of their language. Missionaries translated the treaty. It was called Te Tiriti o Waitangi, or the Treaty of Waitangi.

On February 6, 1840, about 40 chiefs signed the treaty. Then, it was copied and taken around the country. About 500 other people signed it. Most signed the Māori version.

William Hobson (right) and Māori chiefs signing the Treaty of Waitangi.

Some English words had no exact equivalent in the Māori language. In the English version, Māori gave "all the rights and powers of sovereignty" to the British Crown. They were guaranteed "undisturbed possession" of their lands, forests, fisheries, and other places. But in the Māori version, "sovereignty" was translated into "kawanatanga katoa," which means government. The word used for "possession" was "tino rangatiratanga," which means chieftainship. That gave the Māori and English different ideas about what they were signing.

Having one treaty in two languages created problems. Māori lost much of their land. They lost access to food sources in forests and rivers. They could no longer use places like burial sites that were deeply important to them. Cultural practices like traditional healing were banned or discouraged.

Some people hold protests on February 6. In 1975, the government created the Waitangi Tribunal to hear and report on Māori Treaty claims. The Tribunal makes sure the principles and promises laid down in the treaty (including the Māori version) are honored.

Waka ama crew members performed a ceremonial dance called the *haka* during Waitangi Day in 2013.

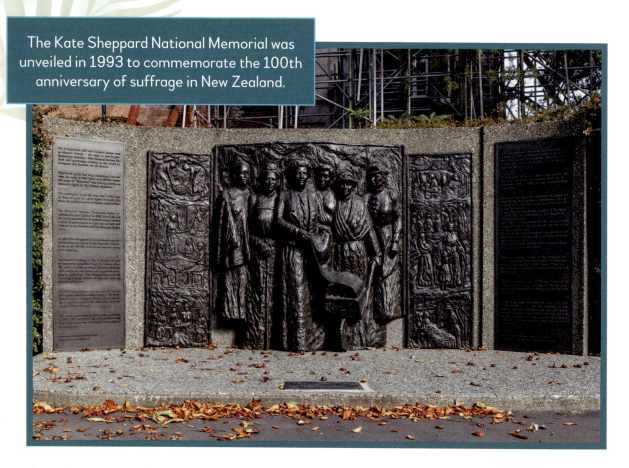

The Kate Sheppard National Memorial was unveiled in 1993 to commemorate the 100th anniversary of suffrage in New Zealand.

Another special day is **Suffrage** Day on September 19. New Zealand was the first country to give women the right to vote. This took years of peaceful protest. Women held meetings and gave speeches. They wrote letters and articles. They signed petitions. The leader of the movement, Kate Sheppard, organized a petition. Thousands of people signed. It was taken to Parliament in 1893 and rolled out like a long carpet. Today, you can see it on display in Wellington.

On September 19, 1893, they won the vote at last. In November, Elizabeth Yates was elected mayor of New Zealand. This made her the first female mayor in the British Empire.

In May 1893, suffragist Meri Te Tai Mangakāhia asked for Māori women to have the right to vote and stand as candidates. This wasn't passed, but she became the first woman to speak in Te Kotahitanga, or the Māori Parliament.

There were no women in the New Zealand Parliament for another 40 years. The first was Elizabeth McCombs in 1933. But by 2001, women held the top five positions in New Zealand. The governor-general and prime minister were both women.

Famous Firsts

Voting rights for women is only one of New Zealand's firsts. It was one of the first countries that gave older people a **pension**.

It was also one of the first countries with an eight-hour working day. Samuel Parnell arrived in Wellington in 1840. He was a carpenter. At that time, people worked very long hours. Samuel said he would only work for eight hours a day. There weren't many carpenters, so his boss had to agree. Today, there is a public holiday called Labor Day in October. It celebrates the laws that protect workers.

Anzac Day is an important day. It is on April 25. *Anzac* stands for "Australian and New Zealand Army Corps."

Anzac troops helped fight during World War I (1914–1918). On April 25, 1915, they landed at Gallipoli in Turkey. They built trenches and lived in huts and dugouts on the steep hillsides. For eight months, they tried to fight their way past the Turkish troops. They never made it more than a few miles inland. Today, there are many graves of New Zealand soldiers in cemeteries at Gallipoli.

Anzac Day is to remember everyone who has served or died in war. Some people get up and go to a dawn service. There are other services later in the day. Many towns and cities have a war memorial. Anzac Day services are often held there. People wear poppies. They bring wreaths to put on the war memorial.

New Zealanders have fought in the South African Wars and both World Wars. They went to Korea and Vietnam. But they have also served as peacekeepers.

Pounamu is also connected with peace. Māori gave each other special pieces of pounamu as a symbol of peace. Pounamu was also an idea that could help bring about peace. Peace agreements were called a *tatau pounamu* (greenstone door). The greenstone door was strong and long-lasting. People hoped that peace would also last a long time too.

The Devonport Naval Base Memorial Wall Service of Remembrance is a Naval memorial for members of the Royal New Zealand Navy who lost their lives while in service.

Kites of the past were made from bark cloth or leaves. They were decorated with carvings, feathers, shells, and paint. Today, there are many different designs made from modern materials.

Matariki, the Māori New Year, falls during winter in June or July. During this time, a group of stars called Matariki can be seen in the sky just before sunrise. They are also called the Pleiades. One creation story says that they are a mother and her daughters. In 2022, Matariki was first celebrated as a public holiday.

In Māori tradition, kites are flown as a way of connecting heaven and earth. They are a symbol to send messages to people who live far away or have died. It is also a time to be grateful for food and the harvest. Families and friends gather for a meal. Matariki is also a time to think about the year ahead.

Some *iwi* (tribes) have a different celebration for Māori New Year. They can't see Matariki clearly from where they live. They look for another star called Puanga. It is also known as the star Rigel, in the Orion constellation.

New Zealand is diverse, and so are its celebrations. Polynesians celebrate the Pasifika Festival. It lasts for three days. There is music, dancing, and fashion. Markets sell food and crafts from the Pacific Islands.

Chinese New Year, Diwali, and Eid are big festivals. Others are quite small. The Blessing of the Boats is an Italian tradition. Local ministers sail out to bless the boats. They pray for the boats to stay safe and catch lots of fish.

New Zealand is small. But the people use their voices to speak up.

The Māori Land March took place in 1975. It began with 50 people who protested the continuing losses of Māori land. At the front was Whina Cooper, a respected leader. She was nearly 80 years old. The march began at the top of the North Island and went for 621 miles (1,000 kilometers). Around 5,000 people arrived in the capital of Wellington. The Land March brought awareness to the issue. Thousands signed a petition to protest too. In 1981, Cooper was granted the title Dame. This is a title given by the Crown for services to Māori and the community.

Local people joined the Māori Land March as it moved across the island.

In 1981, the South African rugby team arrived in New Zealand. At the time, there was **apartheid** in South Africa. Some people just wanted to watch rugby and thought sports had nothing to do with politics. Others thought supporting the game supported apartheid. Police, protesters, and rugby fans faced each other. A plane dropped smoke bombs over the field. They wanted to stop play. These protests inspired people in South Africa. Nelson Mandela was elected president of South Africa after apartheid ended in 1994. He thanked the New Zealand protesters for their stand.

Waitangi Day protests are used to discuss the Treaty of Waitangi and Māori land loss.

The Ihumātao land was taken from Māori in the 1860s. In 2016, there were plans to turn it into a housing subdivision. Protesters tried to stop this from happening. It gained massive attention in 2019. The New Zealand government finally purchased the land in 2020 to return to the local iwi. This protected the heritage status of the land for all New Zealanders to appreciate.

CHAPTER 4
New Zealand Today

New Zealand is home to people from many countries and cultures. But Māori are the people of the land.

Before the first Europeans arrived, Māori had no name for themselves. They were the only people. They didn't need a name. Then, they started to use the word *Māori*, which meant "normal" or "ordinary." New Zealanders who are not Māori or Pasifika are called *Pākehā*.

New Zealanders are also called Kiwis, after the bird. Kiwis as people are often described as friendly and casual. They like to solve problems. They are resourceful and practical. Kiwis travel a lot. One million New Zealanders live overseas.

Planes, cruise ships, and yachts bring people to the islands. In 2019, there were more than three million visitors. New Zealand's population is only five million.

A hiking trail lets visitors experience New Zealand's grasslands, lakes, and mountains.

Rock pools are fun to swim in and explore.

New Zealand is a long way from anywhere else. The nearest big country is Australia, which is three hours away by plane. It takes about three hours to get to Tonga and six hours to Sāmoa. The Americas and Europe are even farther away.

New Zealanders are proud of their beautiful country. They are open-minded. They welcome people from any background and religion. And people are welcome to come and experience Māori culture.

The climate is mild and the land is full of variety. It's not surprising that many people love the outdoors. In summer, they go boating, **tramping**, and camping. In winter, they ski or snowboard. Some want to look at the wildlife. They go whale watching, swim with dolphins, and listen for kiwi at night. There are cafés to visit, rugby games to watch, and concerts to attend. They visit art galleries and museums. They read, listen to music, play video games, and follow fashion.

Many people want to visit the places where their favorite movies were filmed. Others visit the Dark Sky Reserves. These are areas where the night sky is clear and free from light pollution. Huge numbers of stars can be seen.

Waipu Caves on the North Island are full of bioluminescent insects called glow worms.

DID YOU KNOW?

In 1984, postal worker Naida Glavish answered phones in Māori by saying "kia ora" instead of "hello" in English. She risked being fired, but she wouldn't back down. In 2011, she was recognized for her services to Māori and the community. Today, many people say kia ora in greeting. Glavish was given the title of Dame in 2018.

For a long time, there was one main language with many dialects. Today, it is called te reo Māori. The language wasn't written down. But Māori passed on their knowledge and history in other ways. Songs, prayers, and **proverbs** were a few ways. Stories and legends, genealogy, and the arts were others.

Whānau is the Māori word for family, but it also includes physical, emotional, and spiritual relationships.

Some of the first Europeans learned te reo. They wrote it down and made dictionaries. But then, English became the main language. Māori children were punished if they spoke te reo at school. But the language did not disappear.

Today, te reo Māori is valued. It is taught in many schools. Some schools teach all their classes in te reo. Many adults go to te reo classes. Every year, te reo Māori is celebrated during Māori Language Week in September.

English is still the most common language. But te reo Māori and New Zealand Sign Language are also official languages.

Traditional Māori performing arts are taught to people of all ages.

DID YOU KNOW?

In 1999, the All Blacks were playing in the Rugby World Cup in England. Before one of the games, Hinewehi Mohi sang the New Zealand national anthem in te reo Māori. People were surprised. Some were shocked. But thousands of people heard her on television. Because of Hinewehi's courage, it is now common to sing the national anthem in both languages.

Today, people can take classes to learn how to carve pounamu.

Pounamu is still central to New Zealand's culture and geography. For many years, the art of carving pounamu was lost. But about 50 years ago, a carving school was set up. Seven men were in the first class. Today, many carvers work with pounamu. In 1997, the government gave back the ownership of pounamu to the Ngāi Tahu people. They are now its *kaitiaki* (guardians).

Tourists can look for pounamu on the beaches. But they can only take what can be easily carried or fit into a backpack. Pounamu is often a gift, not something bought for yourself. Every member of the 2020 New Zealand Olympics and Paralympics teams received pounamu pendants.

Pounamu can be a special touchstone known as *kōhatu mauri* (life essence). It sits at the entrance to a building or space. The stone is touched on arrival or when leaving. The mauri stone connects people to the land and to those who came before. During ceremonies of welcome, the spirit of the mauri stone protects the traditional values of the Māori.

A huge mauri stands at Te Papa, the national museum. People rub watery sand over the surface to remove the outer coating on the boulder. The green color slowly appears through the surface, just as it would in a river.

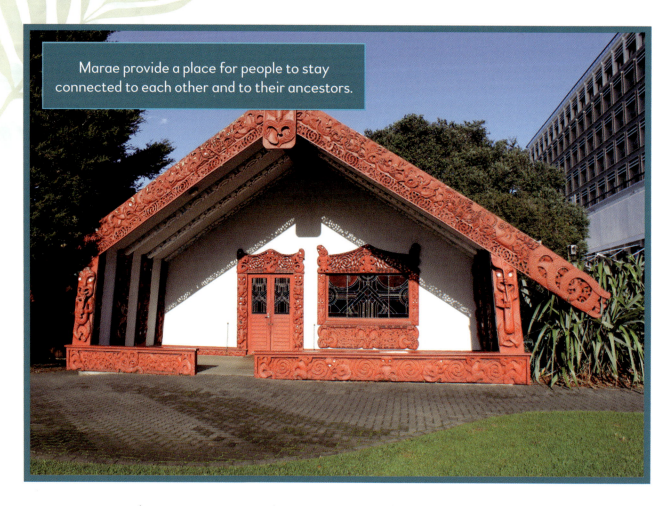

Marae provide a place for people to stay connected to each other and to their ancestors.

The *marae* (meeting grounds) is the center of the Māori community. People gather there for meetings, celebrations, and funerals. Each marae has a courtyard, *wharenui* (meeting house), and *wharekai* (dining hall). There may be other buildings too.

What happens if you are invited onto a marae? Don't worry! Welcoming people is a part of manaakitanga. This means showing hospitality and care toward others. In the *pōwhiri* (welcome ceremony), your hosts will show you what to do.

First, the visitors wait to be greeted and called into the marae. Then, the hosts and visitors take turns to give speeches and sing. Visitors line up to shake hands or press noses with the hosts. Afterward, there will be food. This is part of whanaunatanga, the building of relationships and connections.

You want to respect the Māori culture. How can you do that?

- Respect the language. Find out how to say the names of people and places correctly.
- Learn some common Māori words and phrases.
- Read some stories and legends.
- Learn about proper behavior. For example, the head is *tapu* (sacred). Be careful about touching other people's heads. Don't sit on tables. A table is a place for food.

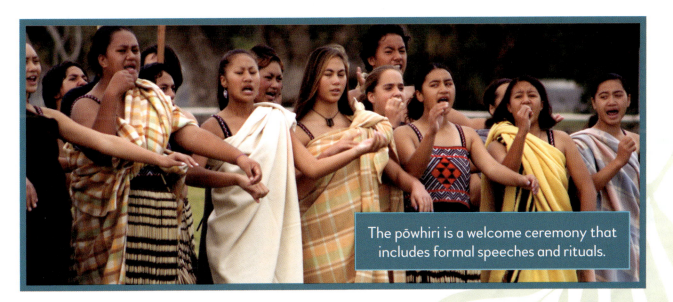

The pōwhiri is a welcome ceremony that includes formal speeches and rituals.

New Zealand has busy towns and cities. But other parts are very remote. You can feel a long way from the 21st century.

It is possible to walk from one end of the country to the other. Te Araroa, or The Long Path, is 1,864 miles (3,000 km) long. It stretches across the North and South Islands. Some people walk from north to south. Others start in the south and head north. You can do it in one session or walk one bit at a time. The whole walk takes about 120 days, or four months.

Some people visit Rēkohu. There is no cell phone coverage there. Rēkohu is even on a different time zone from the rest of New Zealand.

New Zealand looks beautiful through a camera lens too. *Narnia*, *The Lord of the Rings*, *The Hobbit*, and *King Kong* were all filmed there. Good food and good adventures are other reasons people visit. Fruit, vegetables, and seafood are fresh and delicious. Then, you can bungee jump off a bridge or skydive from a plane. Rafting, caving, zip-lining, and **zorbing** are other draws for thrill seekers.

> The Bridge to Nowhere spans the North Island's Mangapurua Gorge. All that remains today is the bridge. There are no roads or buildings on either side.

The Black Ferns are New Zealand's senior women's rugby team.

New Zealand's sports teams are world-class. The team names often include the words *Black*, *White*, *Silver*, or *Fern*. The colors are based on the teams' original uniform colors. The silver fern is used as a national symbol.

Team Names

All Blacks: men's rugby

Black Ferns: women's rugby

Wheel Blacks: wheelchair rugby

Silver Ferns: netball

All Whites: men's soccer

Football Ferns: women's soccer

Tall Blacks: men's basketball

Tall Ferns: women's basketball

New Zealand even has rockets! The launch site is at Mahia on the East Coast of the North Island. People go to the beach to watch the rockets take off. In 2021, Rocket Lab announced it would launch New Zealand's first satellite to the moon.

The country's technology is just as interesting as its geography. Wētā Workshop makes costumes, armor, and props for movies. Another company makes smart collars for cows. The collars are solar powered and work with global positioning systems (GPS). The farmer knows where the cows are and if they are well or sick.

The Wētā Workshop has created props for movies like *Thor: Ragnarok*, *Ghost in the Shell*, and *Pacific Rim: Uprising*.

Aoraki/Mount Cook National Park is home to New Zealand's highest mountain.

New Zealand is one of the biggest countries in the Pacific Ocean. It is bigger than Sāmoa, Tonga, or Fiji. But it is still small compared to other countries. It is smaller than the state of California, and about the same size as Colorado.

For such a small place, there are many things to be proud of. New Zealand has amazing scenery. It has dark skies that glitter with stars. It has fascinating wildlife that you can't find anywhere else in the world.

Do you think you might come here one day? You could go on some exciting adventures. You could go swimming and enjoy the beautiful beaches. You could learn more about the Māori culture. Maybe someone will give you your own piece of pounamu.

Proverbs from the People

A *whakataukī* is a Māori proverb. "Ahakoa he iti, he pounamu" is an example. *Iti* means "small." The literal translation is "Although it is small, it is greenstone (precious)."

This whakataukī can be used in many ways. It might be used to talk about something that seems small but has great value. It might describe a speech that is short but filled with emotion. It might be said when giving or receiving a small gift that has been carefully chosen.

Here is a Māori blessing to finish with. It is written especially for people who travel:

Kia hora te marino,

kia whakapapa pounamu te moana,

kia tere te kārohirohi i mua i tō huarahi.

May the calm be widespread,

may the sea glisten like greenstone,

and may the shimmer of summer dance across your pathway.

–Rangawhenua Tawhaki

Te reo Māori Glossary

Remember to check page 3 for tips on pronunciation!

haka: a ceremonial dance

hei matau: pounamu pendant

iti: small

iwi: tribes

kaitiaki: guardians

kia ora: hello

kōhatu mauri: life essence

manaakitanga: hospitality, kindness, and support

marae: meeting grounds

pounamu: greenstone

pōwhiri: welcome ceremony

Rangatira: chief

tapu: sacred

tatau pounamu: greenstone door

waka: canoe

whakataukī: proverb

whānau: family

whanaunatanga: relationship and connection

wharekai: dining hall

wharenui: meeting house

whare whakairo: carved meeting house

English Glossary

apartheid (uh-PAR-tied): a policy of segregation or discrimination based on race

bush (BUSH): thick, mostly uninhabited forest

demigod (DEM-ee-gahd): someone who is part human, part god

indigenous (in-DIJ-uh-nuss): native to an area

migrants (MY-grunts): people who move away from home to another country or place, for work or other reasons

missionaries (MISH-uh-nae-rees): people sent to promote Christianity in a foreign country

pension (PEN-shuhn): money paid by the government to anyone who has stopped working because of age or sickness

proverbs (PROH-vuhrbs): short sayings that give advice or explain some truth about life

suffrage (SUF-ruj): the right to vote in an election

tramping (TRAM-ping): hiking, often for days on end, through rough country

treaty (TREE-tee): a formal written agreement between countries or different sides

zorbing (ZOR-bing): rolling down a hill strapped inside a giant plastic ball, or orb

Read More about the Pacific Islands

Books

Klepeis, Alicia. *New Zealand.* Minneapolis, MN: Bellwether Media, Inc., 2021.

Spanier, Kristine. *New Zealand.* Minneapolis, MN: Jump!, Inc., 2022.

Toumuʻa, Ruth. *Tonga.* Chicago, IL: Norwood House Press, 2023.

Websites

National Geographic: New Zealand (https://kids.nationalgeographic.com/geography/countries/article/new-zealand) Maps, fast facts, photos, and other info about New Zealand.

Rugby Basic Rules for Kids (https://www.rookieroad.com/rugby/basic-rules-for-kids/) Basic rules, equipment information, and a rundown of rugby players and positions.

Speak Māori for Kids! (https://speakmaoriforkids.co.nz/app/) Language lessons for kids who want to learn how to speak Māori.

Index

celebrations, 27, 38
creation stories, 6, 27

dendroglyphs, 14–15

Europeans, 9, 11–12, 18, 30, 34

languages, 4, 20–21, 34–35, 39

Māori, 4–5, 6, 9–13, 20–21, 23–24, 27–29, 30, 32–35, 37–39, 44–45
Moriori, 14

plants and animals, 14, 16–17
pounamu, 5, 8–10, 13, 24, 37, 44–45
protests, 21–22, 28–29

sports, 18, 29, 35, 42
suffrage, 22

Waitangi, 20–21

About the Author

Philippa Werry lives in Wellington, New Zealand. She writes fiction, nonfiction, plays, and poetry for children and young adults. She has a particular interest in history, which has led to titles such as *Anzac Day, Waitangi Day, Armistice Day, The New Zealand Wars*, and *The Telegram*. Her work has appeared in the *New Zealand School Journal*, other educational publications, and various anthologies, and it has been broadcast on radio.

About the Consultant

André Ngāpō is from Aotearoa, New Zealand. He is an award-winning writer with dozens of titles written for children. André is an educator of child and adolescent brain development with Brainwave Trust Aotearoa. He has over 25 years of experience working in schools.